Waterfalls
The Beauty and the Power

To:

From:

I'll drive a hundred miles to see the beauty and power of a waterfall. Watching the water fall and listening to the water hit the pool below can be so calming and mesmerizing. The water drives generators that provide power to many. Enjoy the beauty and also appreciate the power.

~B. T. Robb

There is a waterfall in every dream. Cool and crystal clear, it falls gently on the sleeper, cleansing the mind and soothing the soul.

~ Virginia Alison

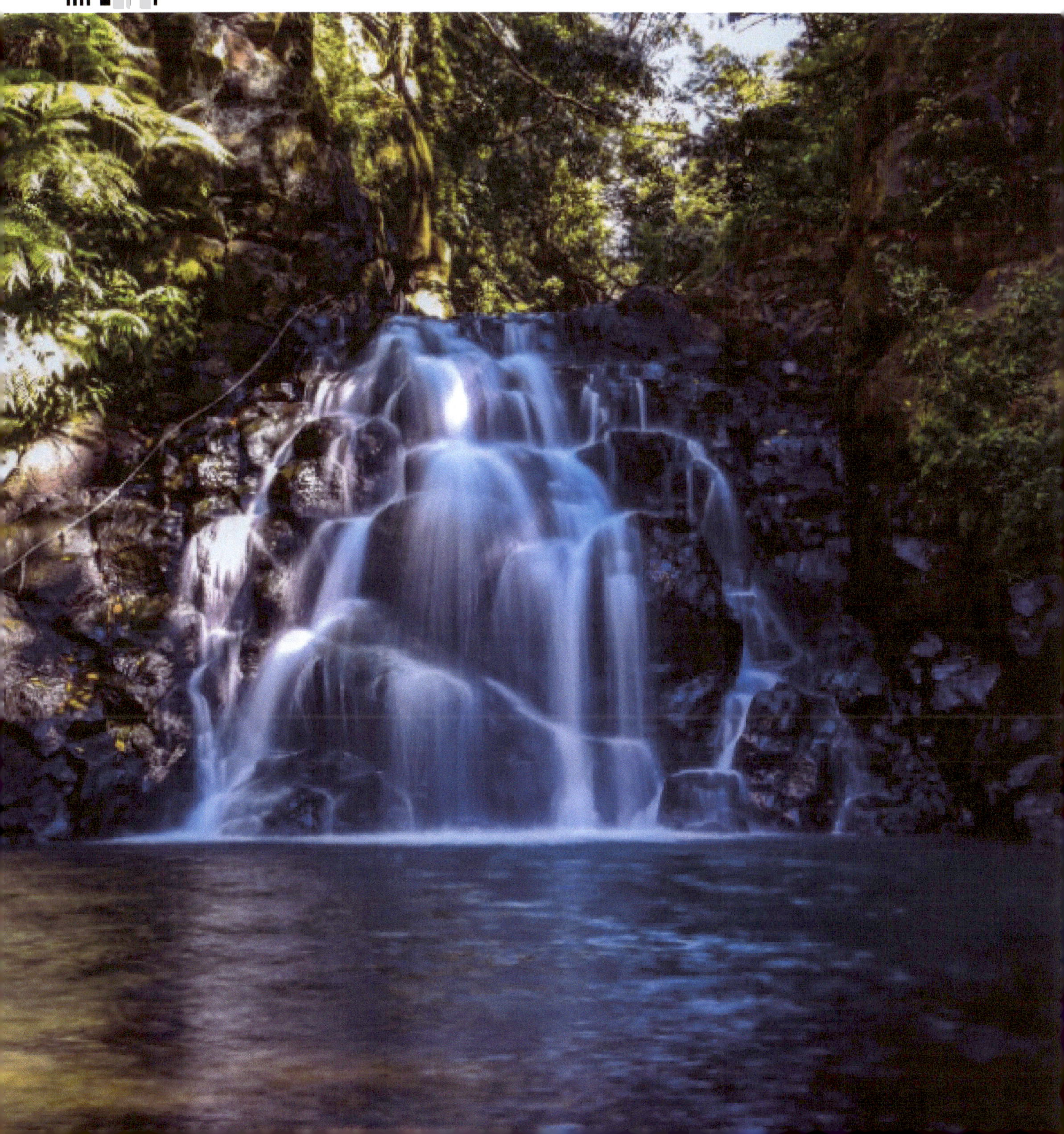

Rivers, water streams, water falls, water lakes, seas and oceans confirm Your creativity.

~ Euginia Herlihy

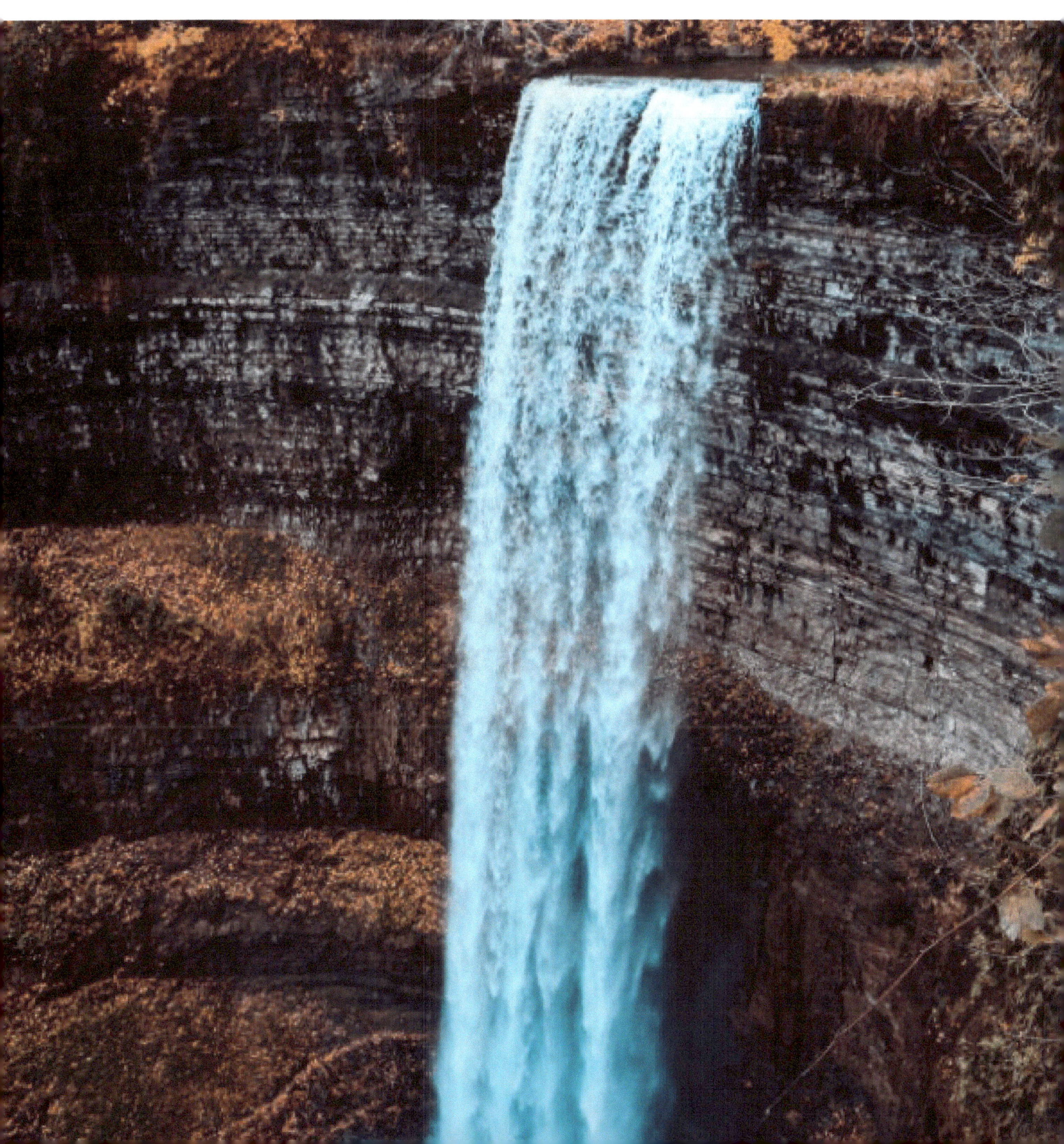

Do not feel sad for your tears as rocks never regret the waterfalls

~ Munia Khan

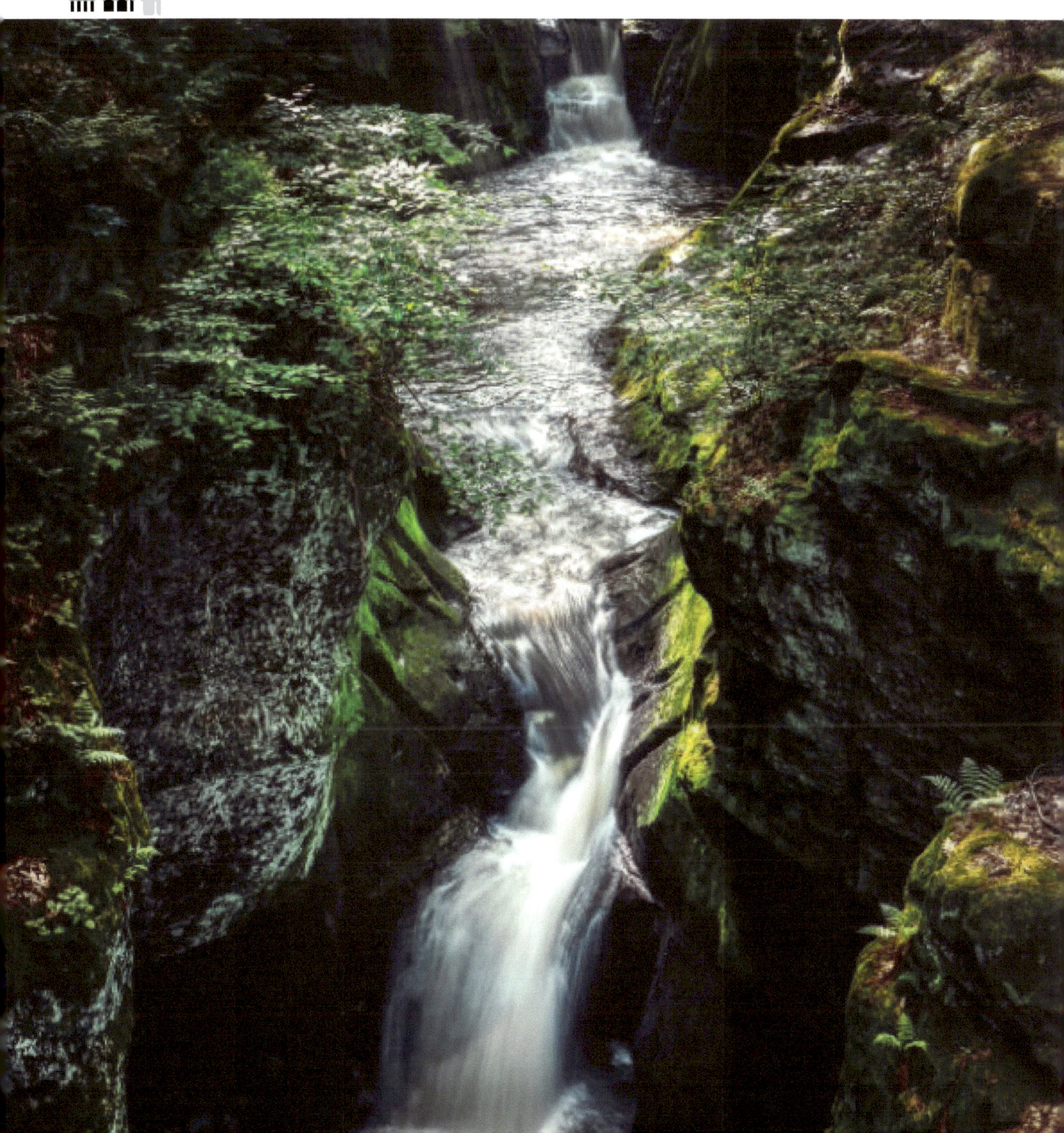

Water is the softest thing, yet it can penetrate mountains and earth. This shows clearly the principle of softness overcoming hardness.

~ Lao Tzu

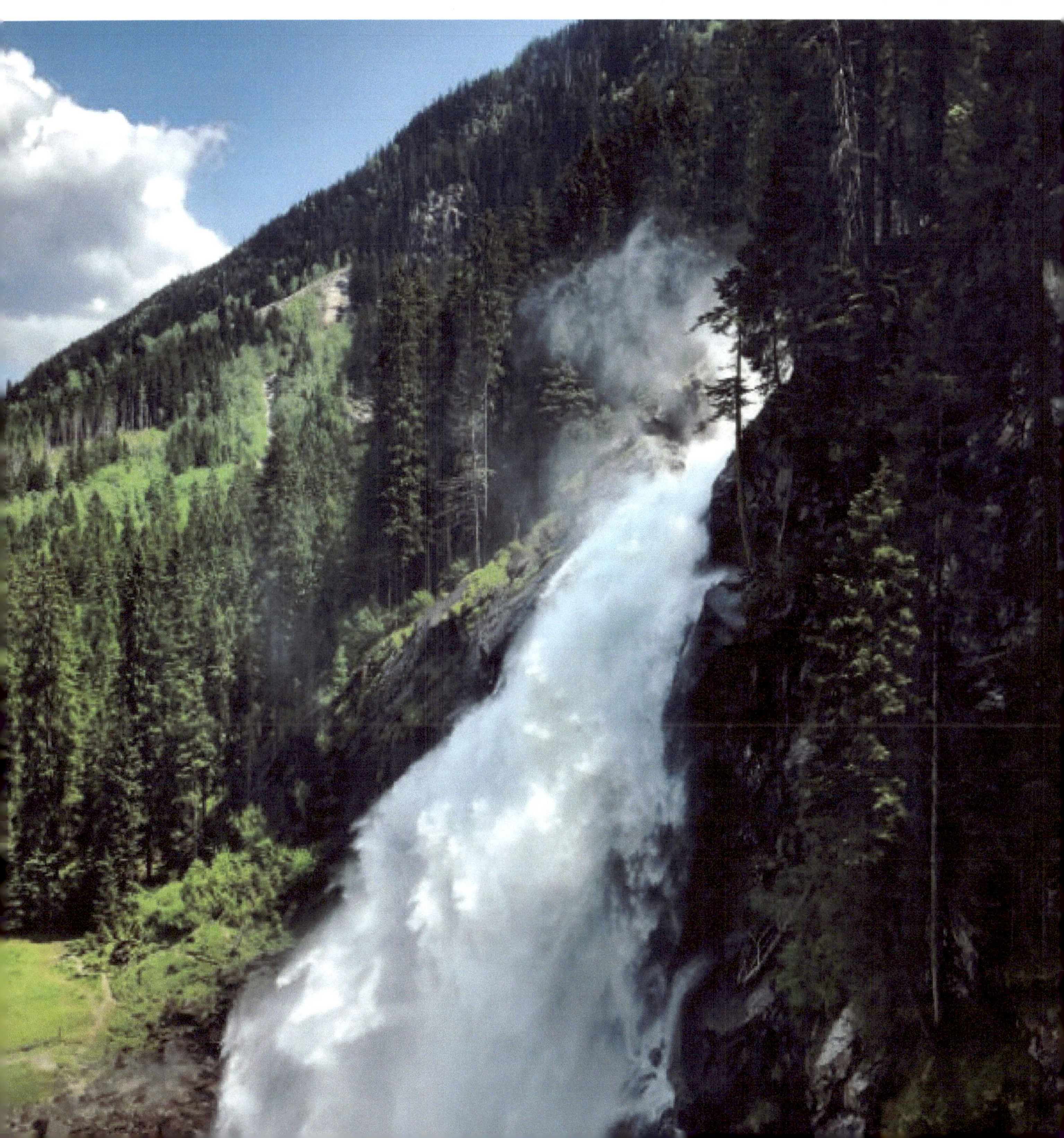

Water is peaceful. I am at rest. In the water, I am safe and pulled in where I can't get out. Everything slows down—the noise and the racing of my thoughts.

~ Jennifer Niven

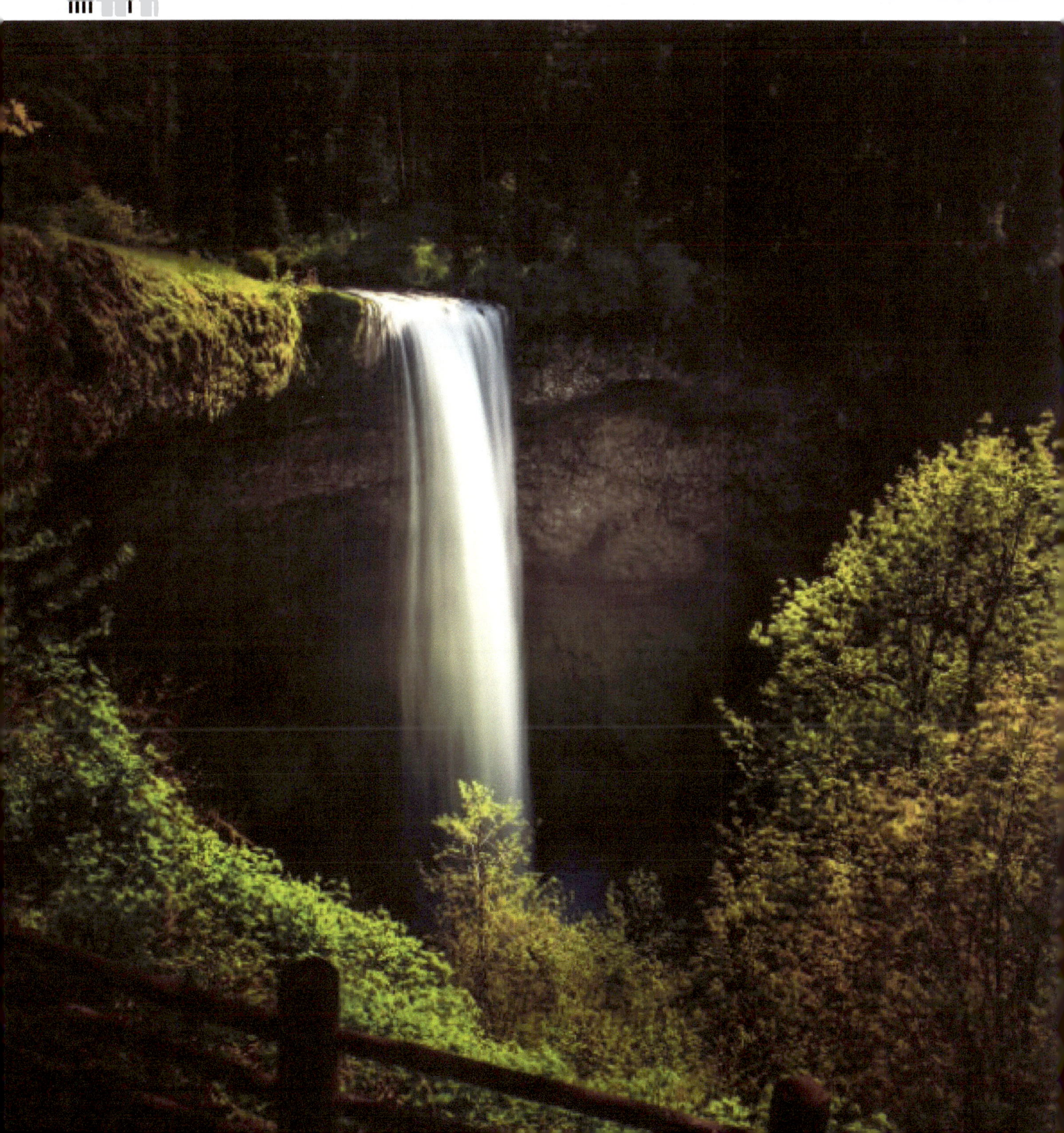

*Water and grace flow to persons
and places that are lower.*

~Shri Radhe Maa

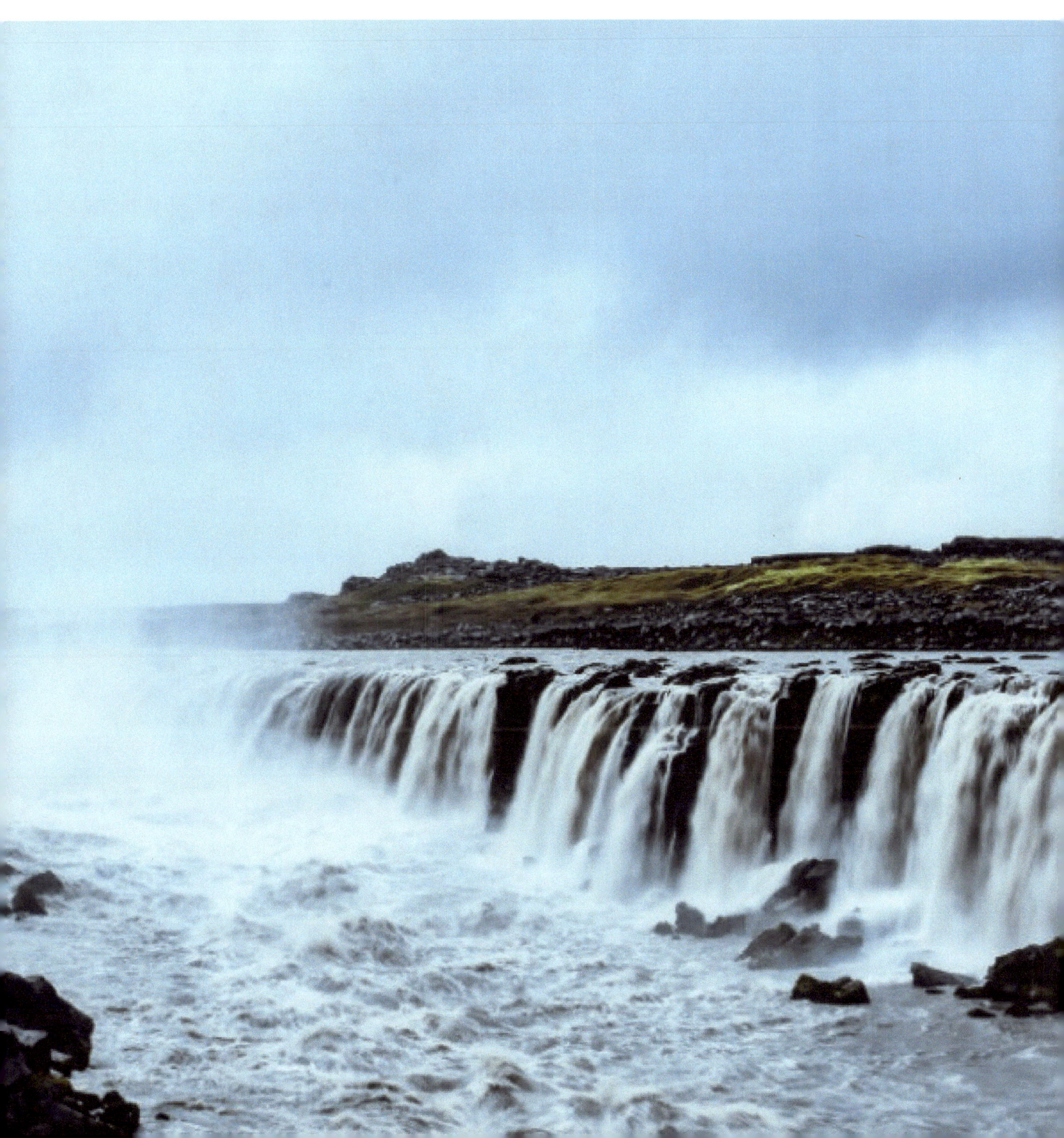

Water is like a child, it always wants to be in motion.

~ Viraj J Mahajan

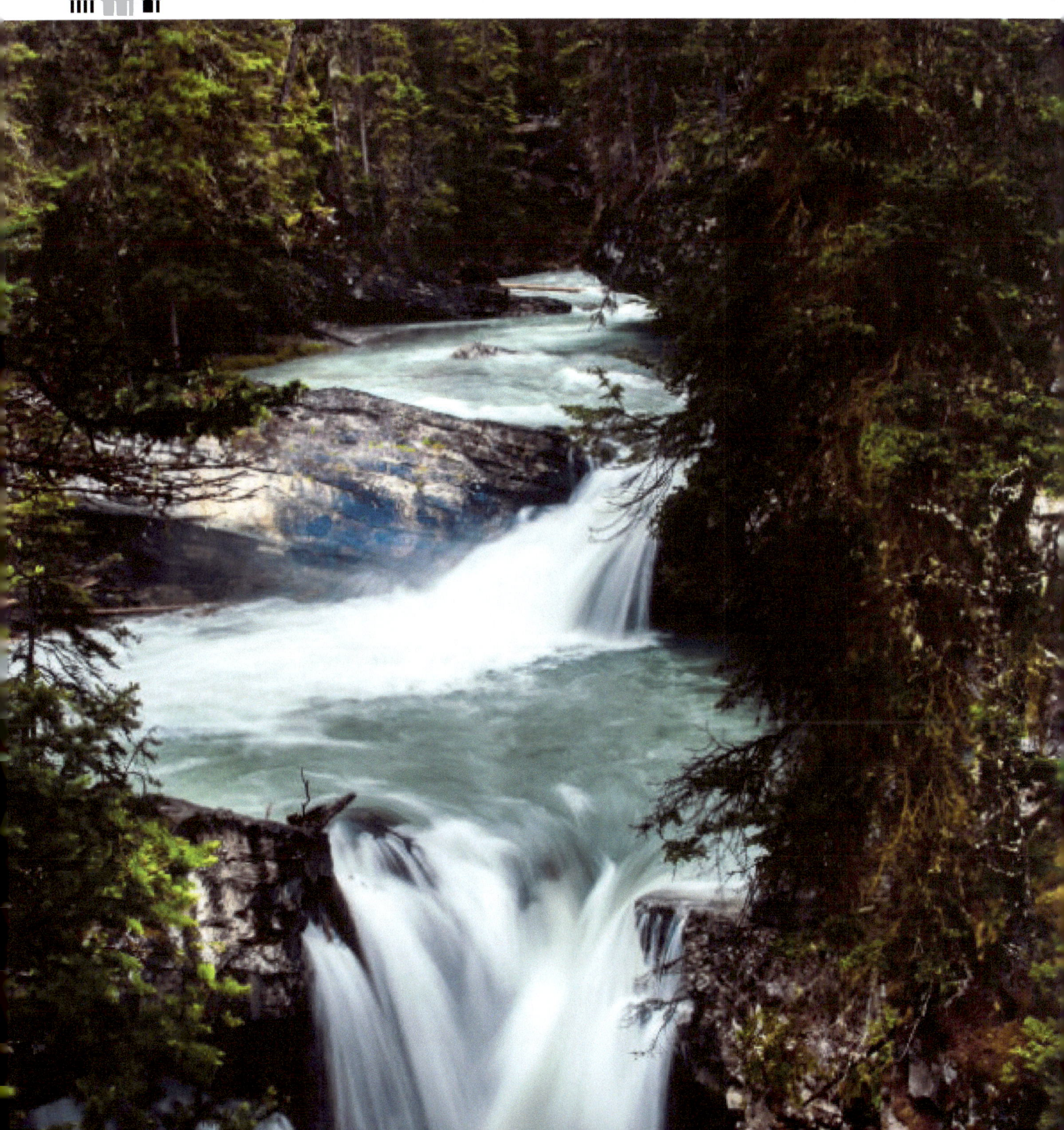

*Water quenches the body; love
quenches the soul.*

~ Matshona Dhliwayo

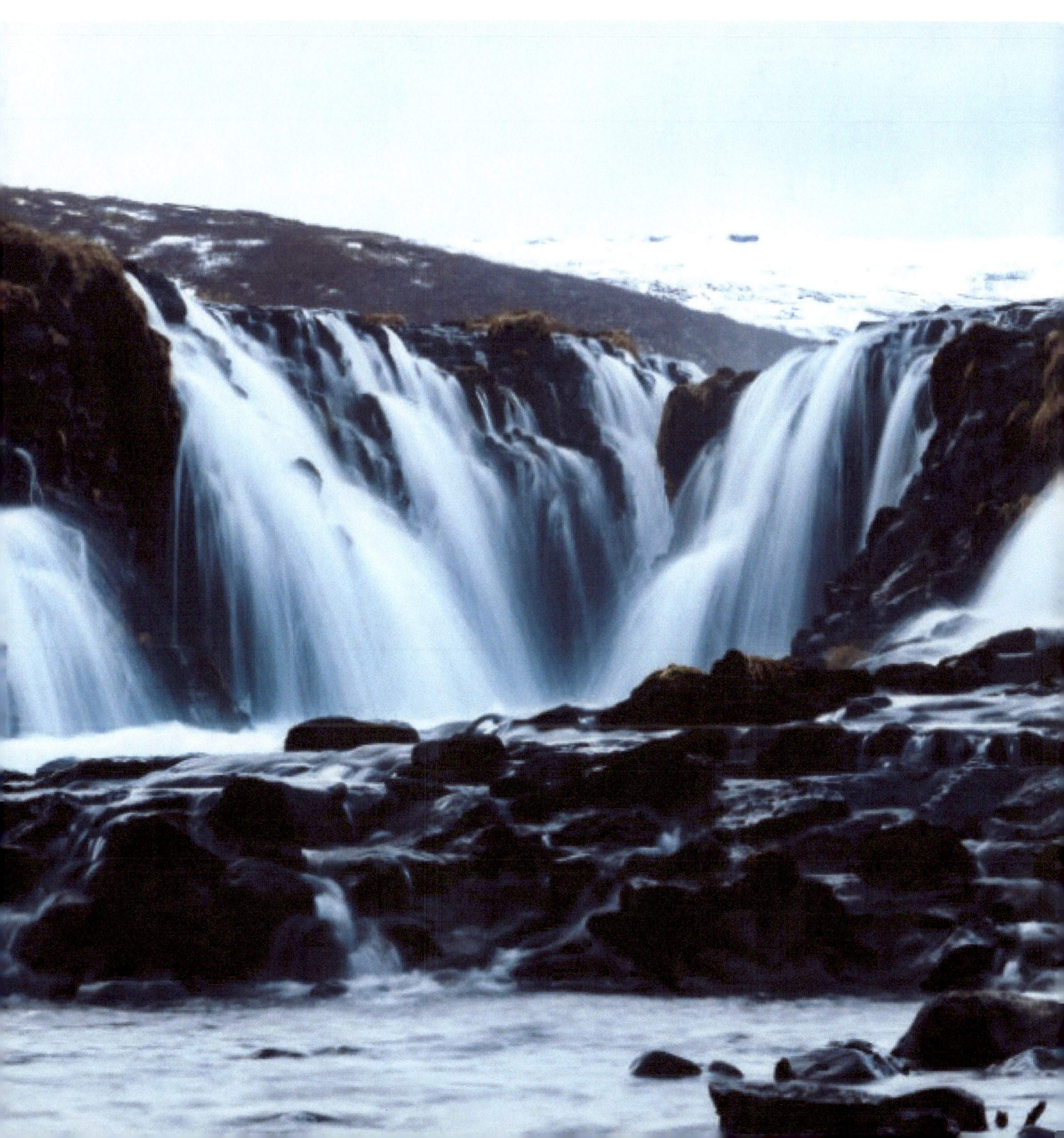

Water has no hands,

but carries great ships.

Air has no shoulders,

but carries large planes.

The Sun has no eyes,

but finds its way around the universe.

~ Matshona Dhliwayo

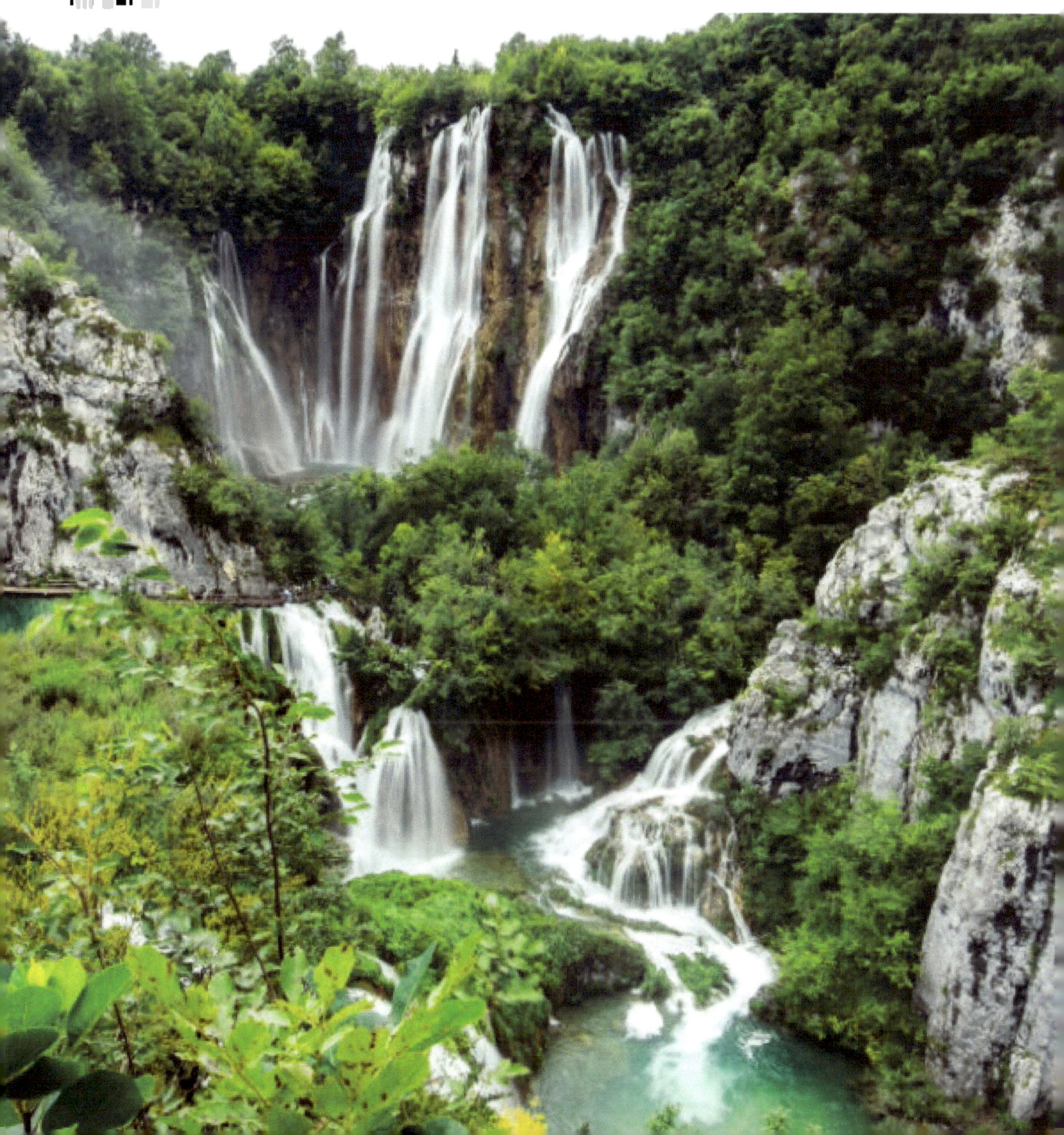

Dripping water hollows out stone, not through force but through persistence

~ Ovid

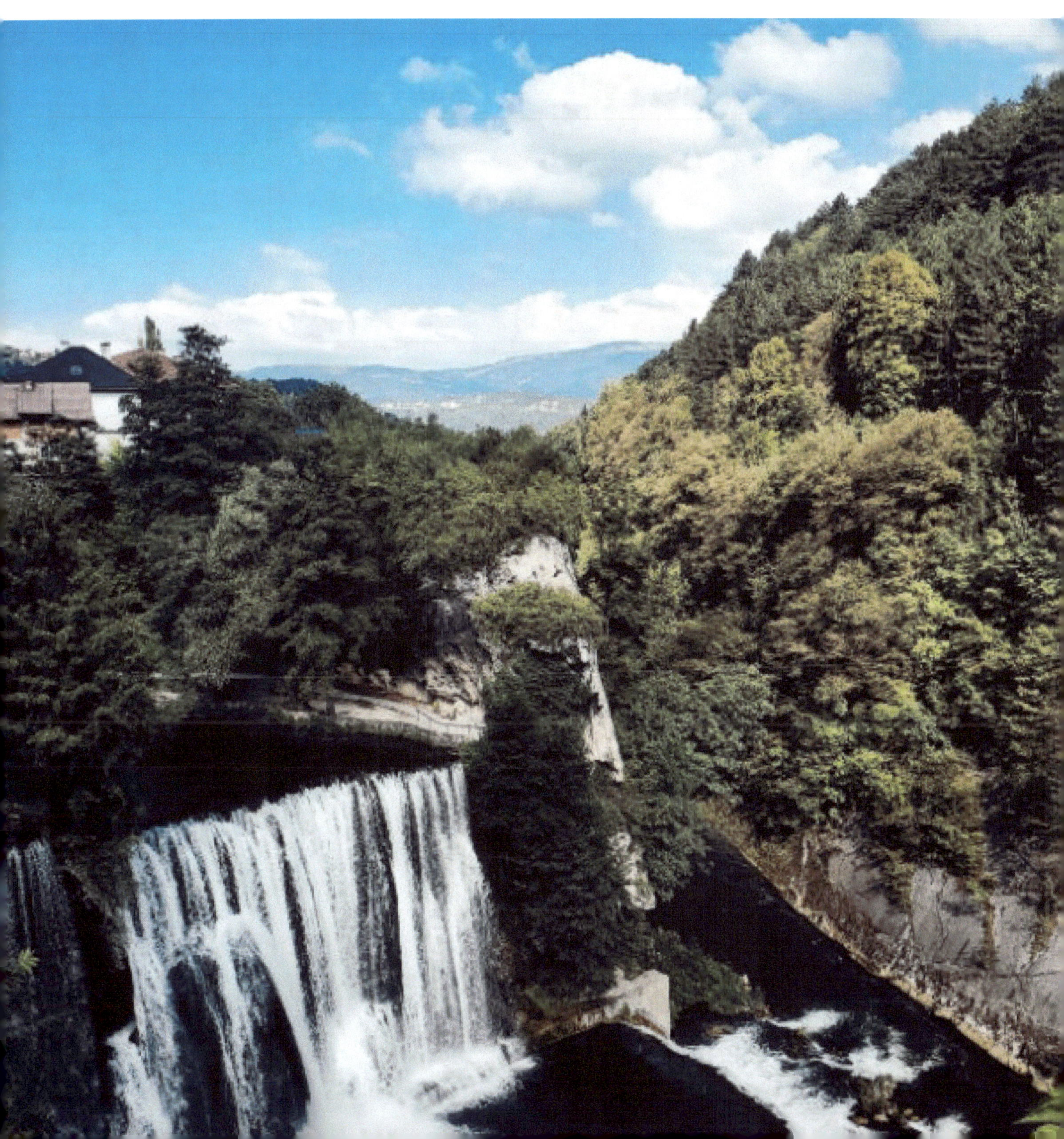

All water has a perfect memory and is forever trying to get back to where it was.

~ Toni Morrison

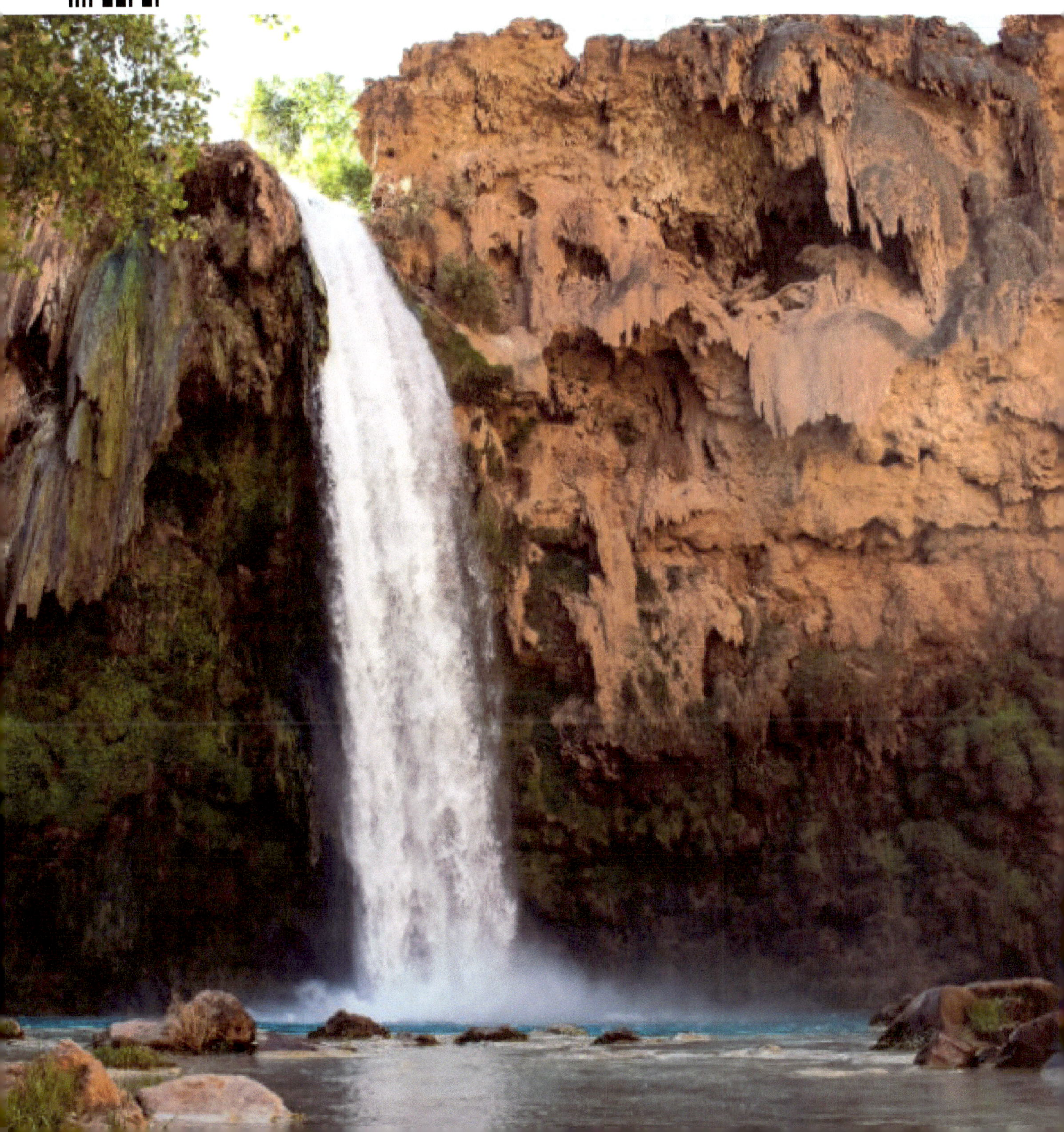

*Even water carves monuments
of stone, so do our thoughts
shape our character.*

~ Hugh B. Brown

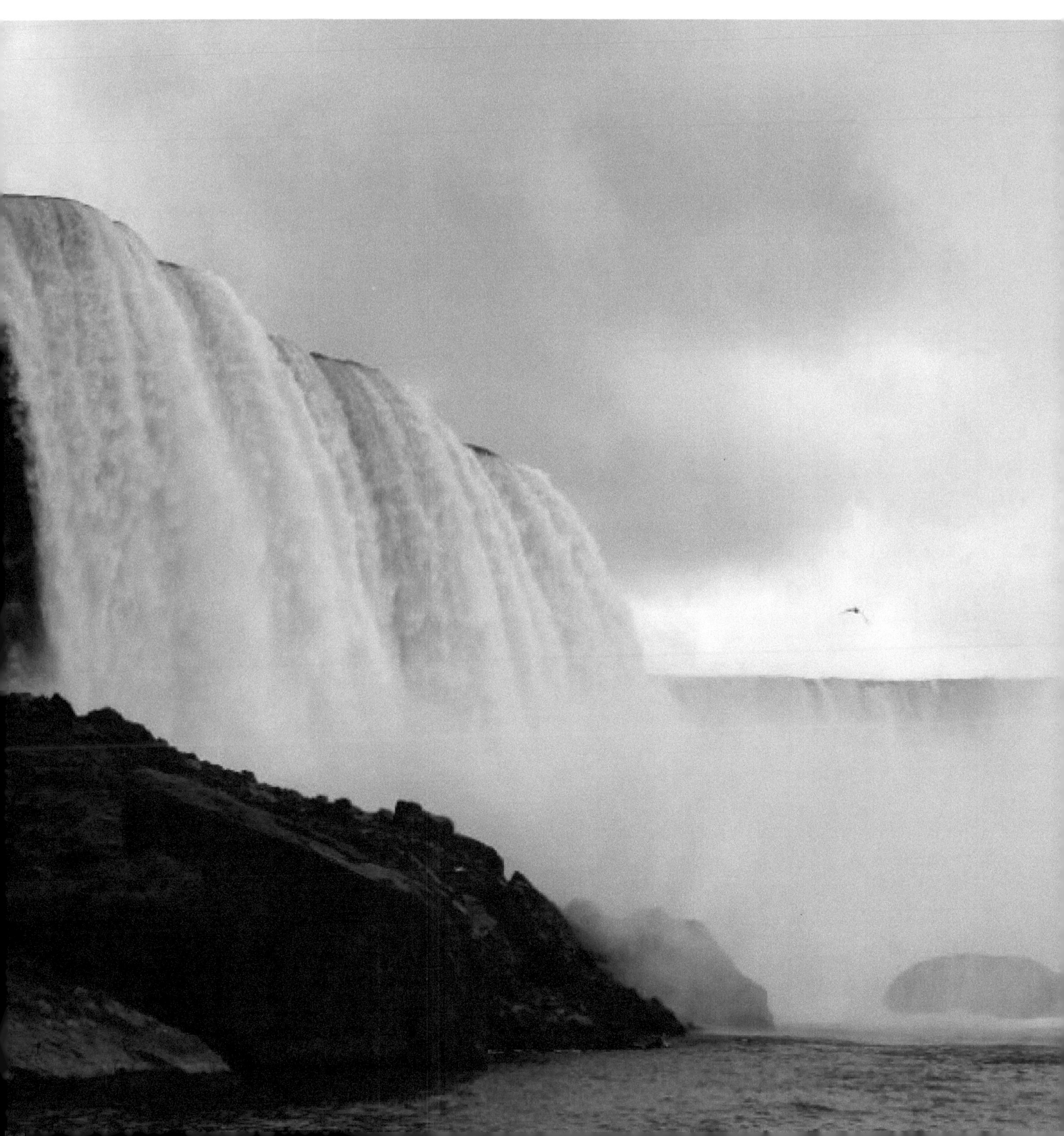

Rivers, water streams, water falls, water lakes, seas and oceans confirm Your creativity.

~ Euginia Herlihy

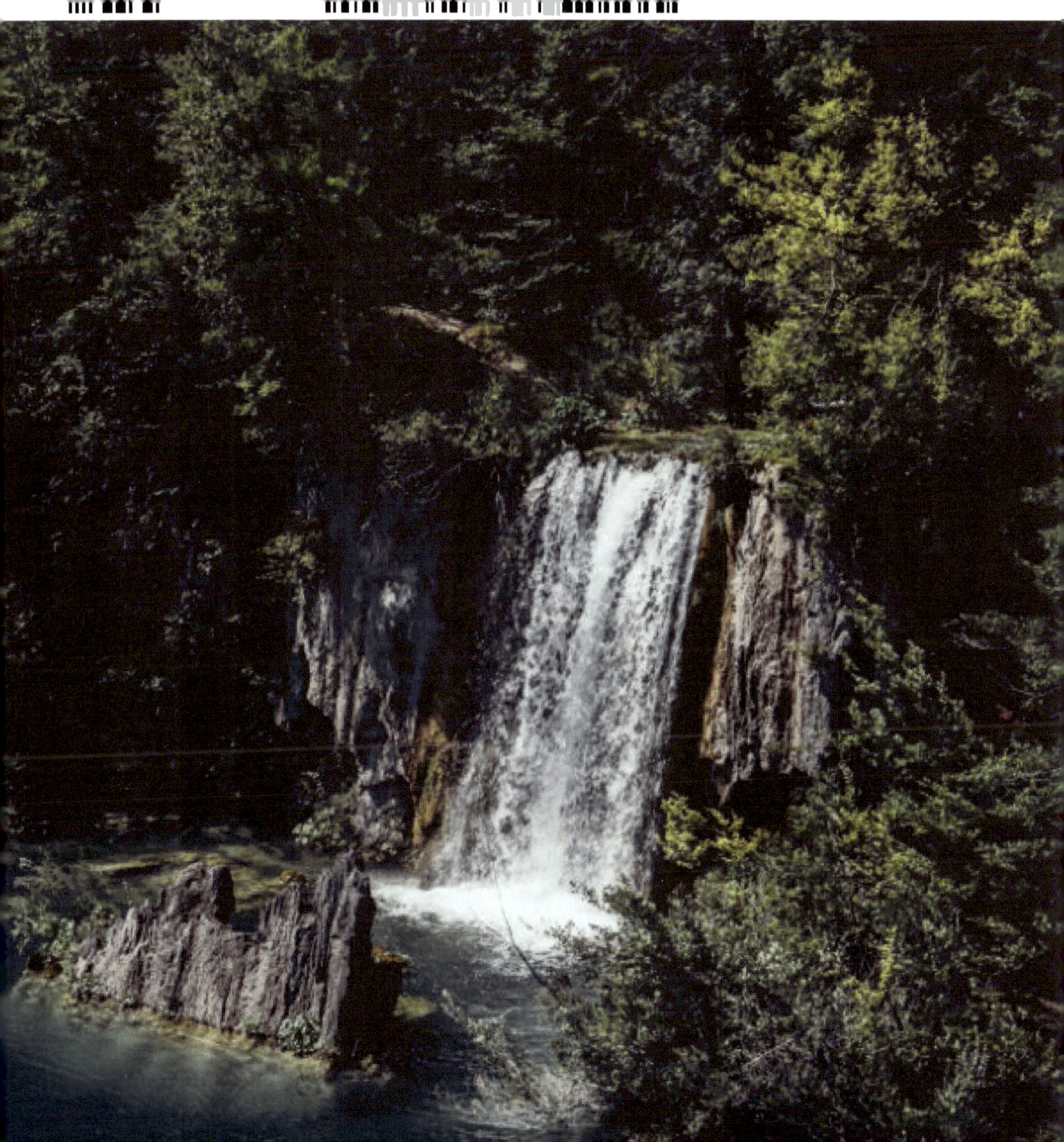

As water is to a thirsty soul so is love to a broken heart.

~ Ikechukwu Izuakor

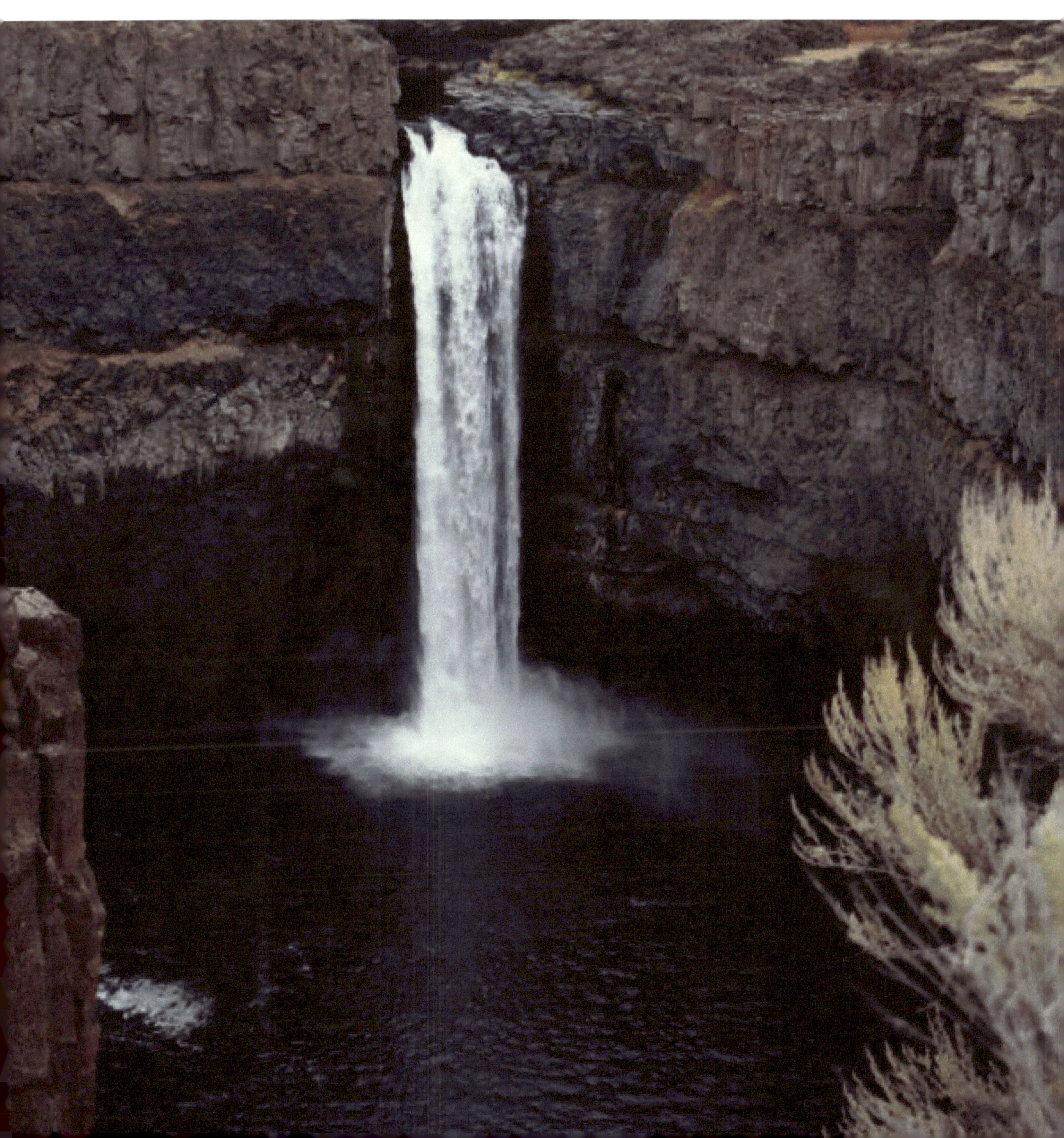

Thoughts, like water, will stay on course if we make a place for them to go. As you learn to control your thoughts, you can gain courage, conquer fear and have a happy life.

~ Boyd K. Packer

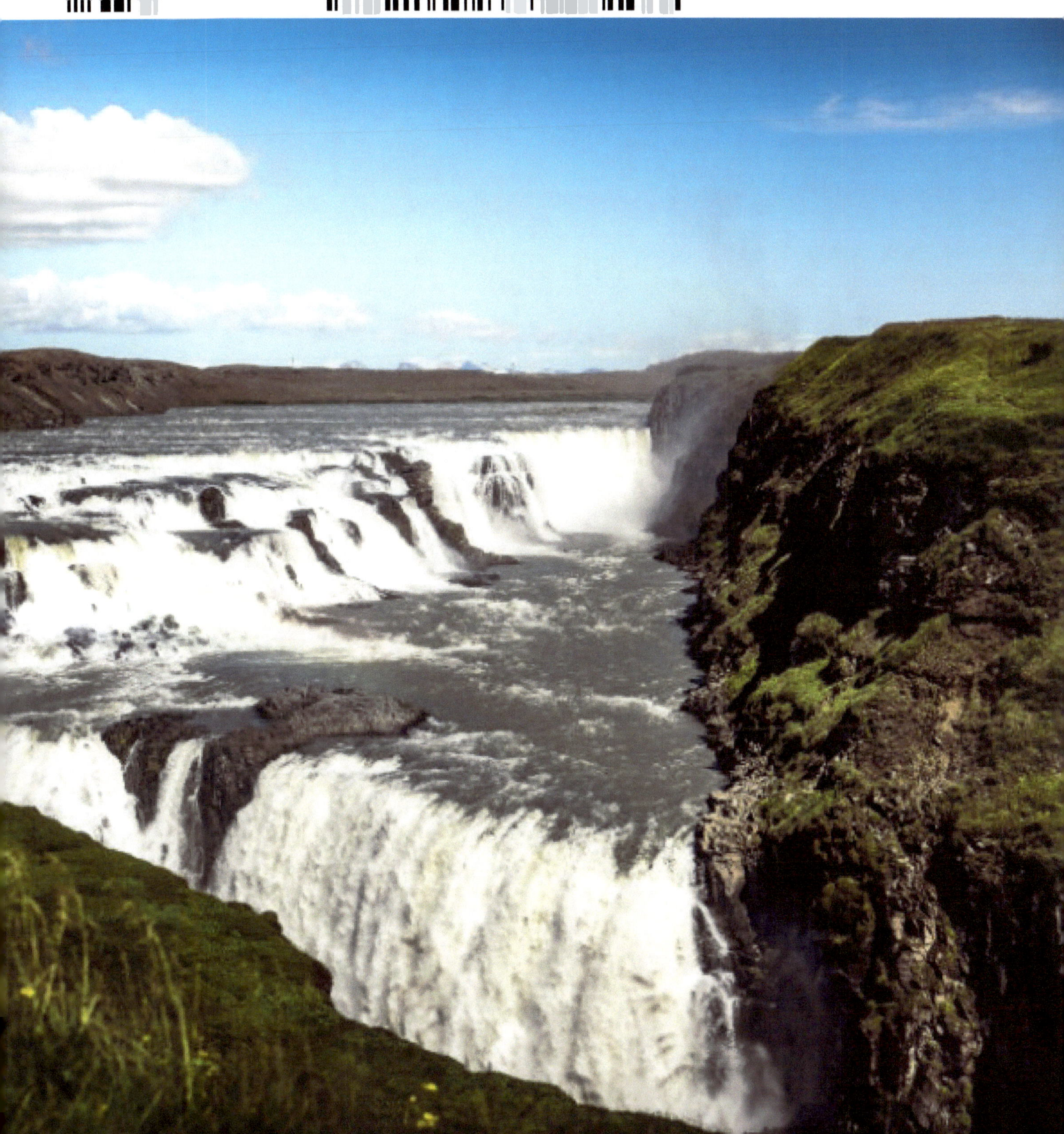

Sunshine and water—the perfect recipe for happiness.

~ Toni Sorenson

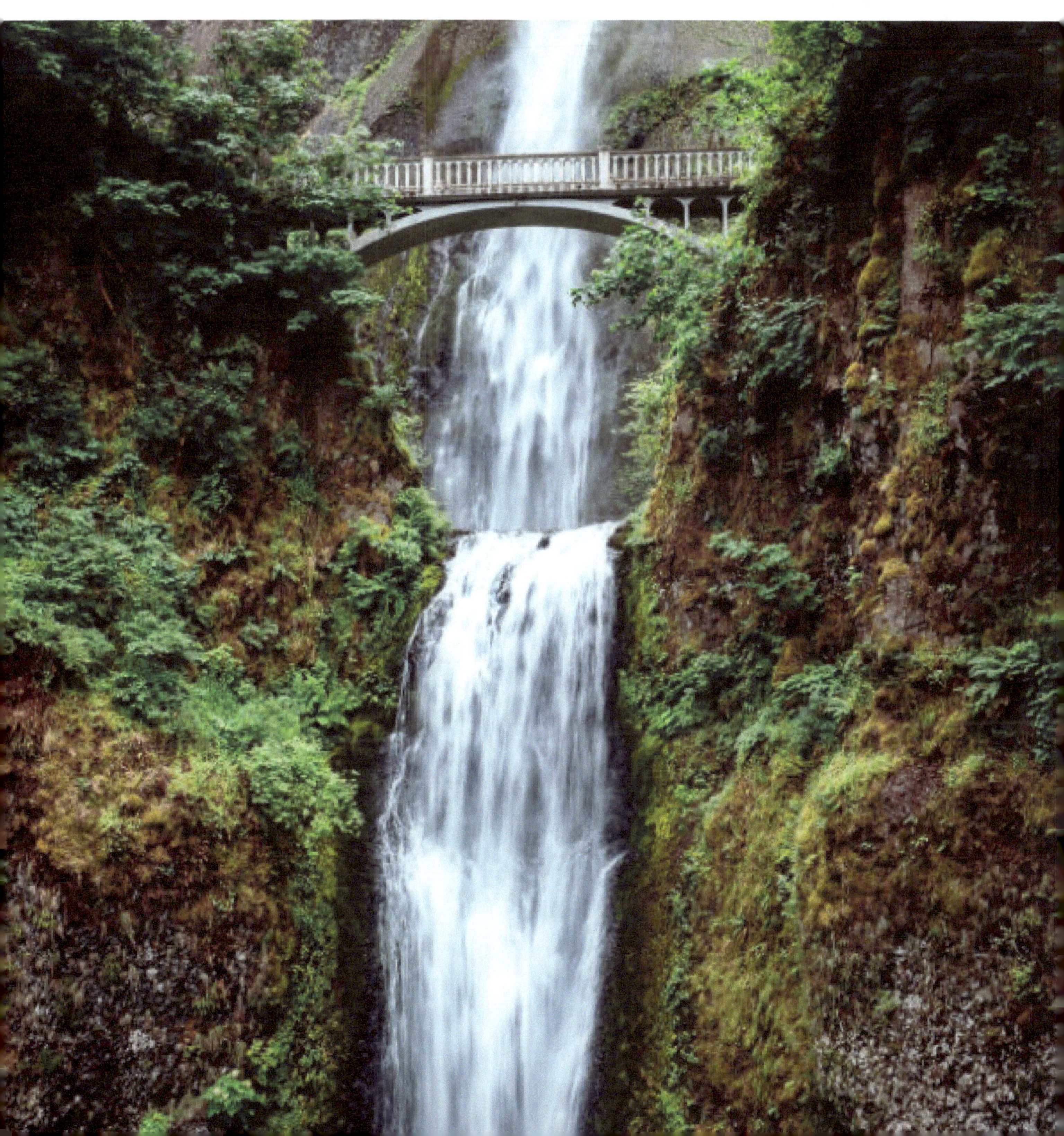

Sunset on the water ought to be a quiet and easy time, but I guess some people can't stand a little silence.

~ Carl Hiaasen

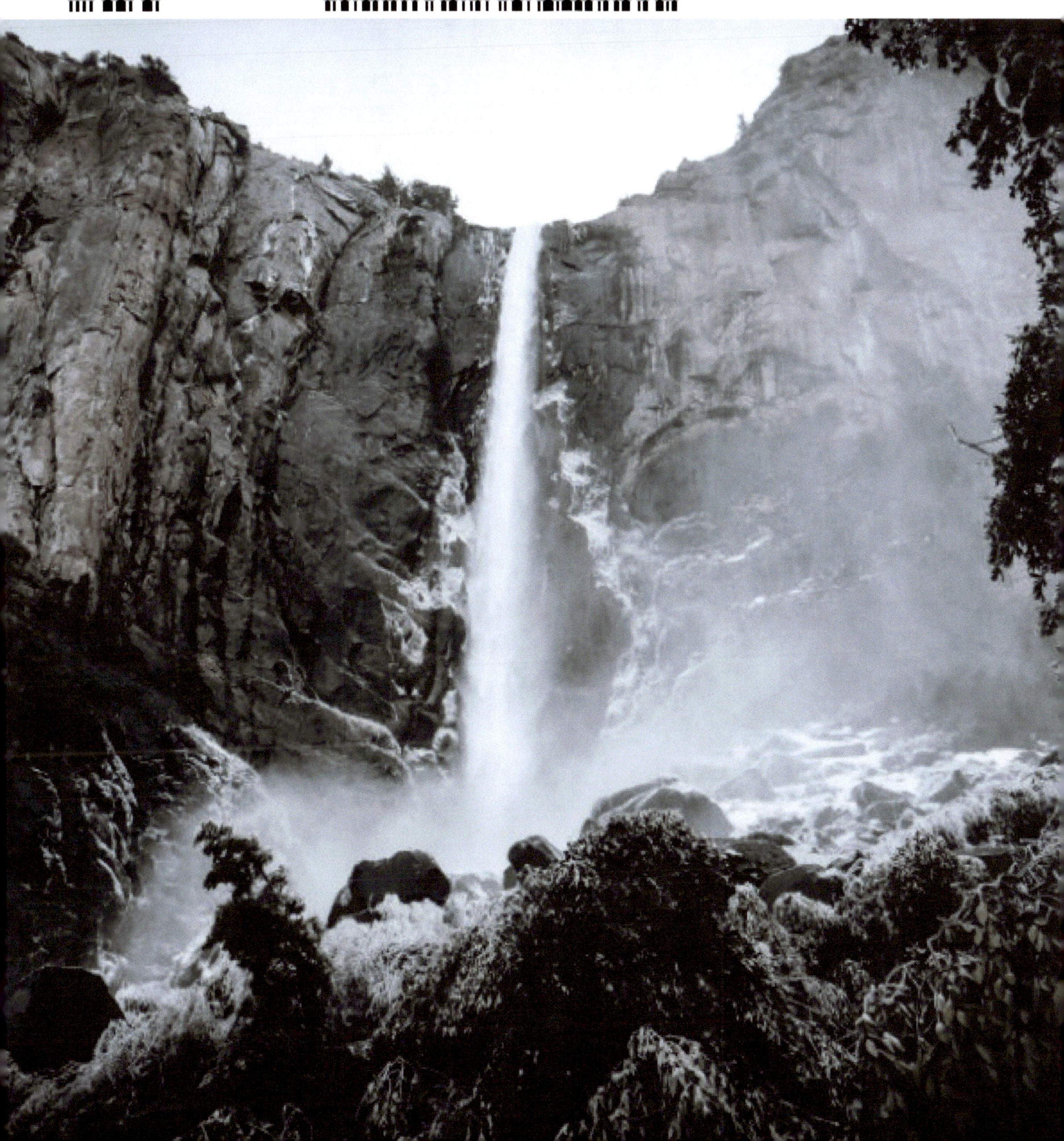

A girl without braids is like a mountain without waterfalls.

~ Roman Payne

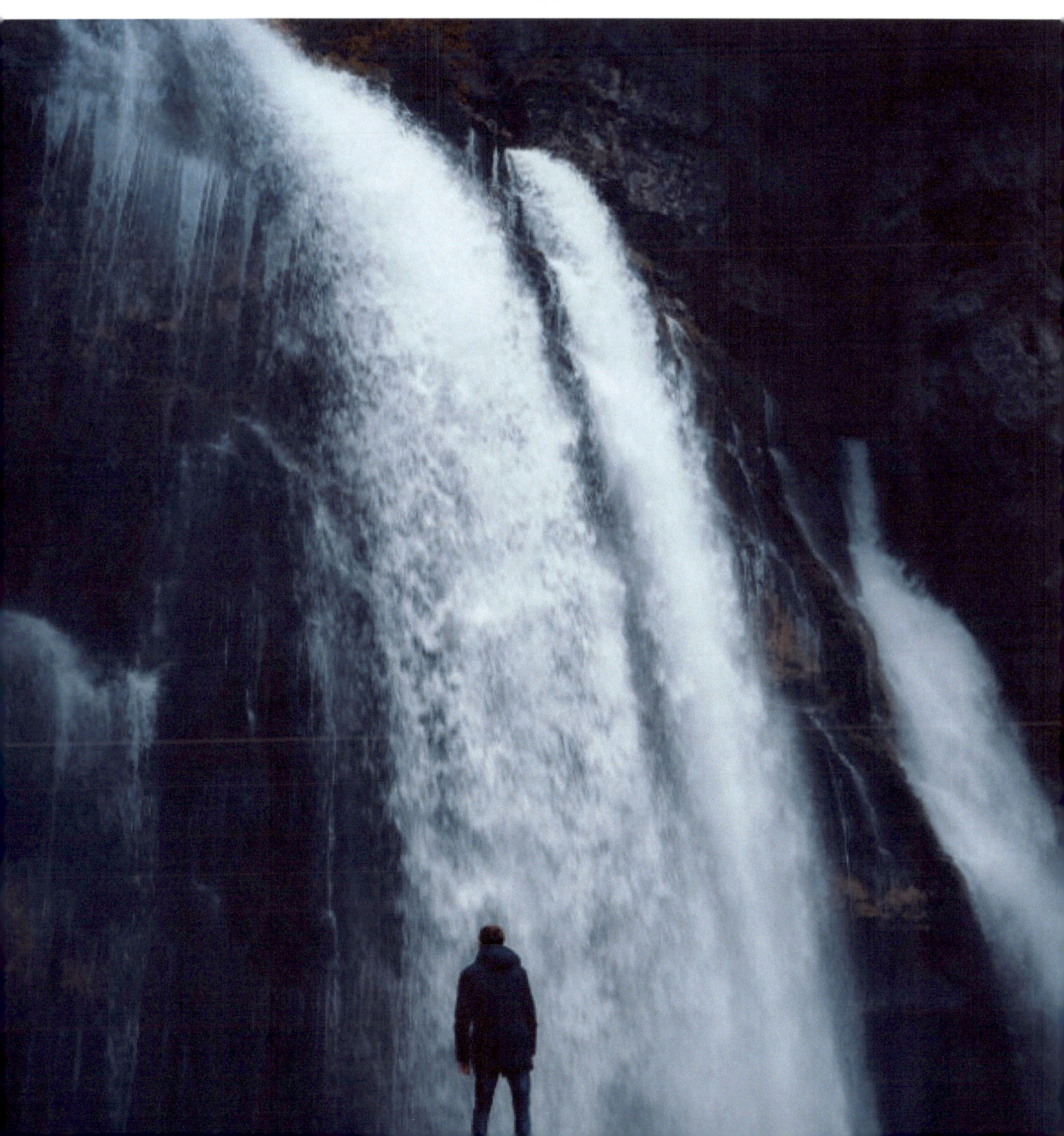